Vision Quality is based on providing a level of Excellence, Unparalleled Professional Service and Craftsmanship driven by our Culture and our People.

VISION TECHNOLOGIES

Making Vision Reality

We hope this book inspires you to promote and support OUR Vision!

January 2011

vision

These quotations were gathered lovingly but unscientifically over several years and/or contributed by many friends or acquaintances. Some arrived, and survived in our files, on scraps of paper and may therefore be imperfectly worded or attributed. To the authors, contributors and original sources, our thanks, and where appropriate, our apologies. —The Editors

CREDITS

Compiled by Dan Zadra
Designed by Steve Potter

ISBN: 978-1-932319-40-8

3rd Printing. 10K 06 10

Printed in China

A vision is a target that beckons.

WARREN BENNIS & BURT NANUS

EVERY COMPANY
COMES WITH
A STORY,
AND THE POSSIBILITY
OF A GREAT
ADVENTURE.

BENJAMIN WALLACE

The future cannot be predicted, but futures can be invented. It was (our) ability to invent which has made human society what it is.

DENNIS GABOR

WHERE THERE IS NO VISION,
THE PEOPLE PERISH.

PROVERBS 29:18

If we do not think about the future, we cannot have one.

JOHN GALSWORTHY

It's time to start living
the life we've imagined.

HENRY JAMES

THE FUTURE

IS NOT SOMEPLACE

WE ARE GOING TO,

BUT ONE WE ARE

CREATING.

THE PATHS TO IT ARE

NOT TO BE FOUND,

BUT MADE.

JOHN SCHAAR

A company should stand for something, fulfill a purpose, and contribute something useful—hopefully something special, even wonderful—or it shouldn't bother being a company at all.

DAN ZADRA

The best companies create a vision, articulate the vision, passionately own the vision, and relentlessly drive it to completion.

JACK WELCH

The mind
supplies the idea for
a nation, but what
gives this idea its
sentimental force
is a community
of dreams.

ANDRÉ MALRAUX

I want to work for a
company that contrib-
utes to and is part of
the community. I want
something not just to
invest in. I want some-
thing to believe in.

DAME ANITA RODDICK

Just getting people in the same place at the same time does not produce a team. Community requires a common vision and shared values.

DIANE DREHER

Leaders and
followers are
both following
the invisible leader —
the big idea —
their shared
purpose and values.

DAN ZADRA

IF YOU THINK OF

VISION

AND MISSION

AS AN ORGANIZATION'S

HEAD AND HEART,

THE VALUES IT HOLDS ARE

ITS SOUL.

VICTOR R. BUZZOTTA

Work has to include

our deepest values and

passions and feelings

and commitments,

or it's not work,

it's just a job.

MATTHEW FOX

AN ORGANIZATION'S VALUES

ARE ITS LIFE'S BLOOD.

MAX DEPREE

What people say is

important, what they

do is more important,

but what they value

is most important.

People don't just go to work to acquire, they go to work to become. They don't just go to work to make a living, they go to make a life.

DAN ZADRA

Let's not just talk about our company values, let's put them into action. Let's not just memorize them, let's live them.

RON KENDRICK

WE CAN DO MORE THAN DREAM,
WE CAN IMAGINE.

A R I S T O T L E

Every great

advance...has

issued from a

new audacity

of imagination.

JOHN DEWEY

Imagination is more important than knowledge. Knowledge is limited. Imagination encircles the world.

ALBERT EINSTEIN

At first people refuse to believe that a strange new thing can be done, then they begin to hope it can be done, then they see it can be done—then it is done and all the world wonders why it was not done centuries ago.

FRANCES H. BURNETT

START WITH THE VISION;
SUCCEED WITH THE PLAN.

DR. LARRY CASE

The way I see it,
there are two
kinds of dreams.
One is a dream
that's always going
to be just that…
a dream…
Then there's a dream
that's more than
a dream;
it's like…a map.

ROBERT COOPER

BUSINESS IS AN INSTINCTIVE
EXERCISE IN FORESIGHT.

HENRY LUCE

THE PRINCIPAL MARK
OF GENIUS
IS NOT PERFECTION BUT
ORIGINALITY,
THE OPENING OF NEW
FRONTIERS.

ARTHUR KOESTLER

I shall make

electricity so

cheap that

only the rich

can afford to

burn candles.

THOMAS EDISON

The 20th Century has been the American Century in large part because of great inventors like the Wright brothers. May we follow their flight paths and blaze our own.

BILL GATES

If the future is to remain

open and free, we need

people who can tolerate

the unknown, who will

not need the support of

completely worked-out

systems or traditional

blueprints from the past.

MARGARET MEAD

Set your expectations high; find

men and women whose integrity

and values you respect; get their

agreement on a course of action;

and give them your ultimate trust.

JOHN AKERS

IF YOU ARE WORKING
ON SOMETHING EXCIT-
ING THAT YOU REALLY
CARE ABOUT, YOU DON'T
HAVE TO BE PUSHED.
THE VISION PULLS YOU.

STEVE JOBS

Knowing that we can make a difference in this world is a great motivator. How can we know this and not be involved?

SUSAN JEFFERS

Reality always forms
around commitment.

KOBI YAMADA

COMMITMENT
UNLOCKS THE DOORS OF
IMAGINATION,
ALLOWS VISION,
AND GIVES US THE "RIGHT STUFF"
TO TURN OUR DREAMS
INTO REALITY.

JAMES WOMACK

COMMITMENT IS NEVER AN
ACT OF MODERATION.

KENNETH G. MILLS

The most radical,

powerful act ever

undertaken by any

human being remains

the act of committing

oneself, beyond

reservation, to a worthy

personal mission.

CHRISTOPHER CHILDS

Leaders are visionaries
with a poorly developed
sense of fear and no
concept of the odds
against them.

ROBERT JARVIK

SUCCESS IS SEIZING THE DAY

AND ACCEPTING RESPONSIBILITY

FOR YOUR FUTURE. IT'S SEEING

WHAT OTHER PEOPLE DON'T SEE,

AND PURSUING THAT VISION, NO

MATTER WHO TELLS YOU NOT TO.

HOWARD SCHULTZ, STARBUCKS

OPEN YOUR ARMS TO CHANGE,
BUT DON'T LET GO OF YOUR VALUES.

U N K N O W N

We will compromise on
almost anything, but not
on our Core Values.
The business of business
is to keep the company alive
and breathlessly excited,
to be a force for good for its
customers, and contribute
something of value to
the community.

DAME ANITA RODDICK

Let each of us work to build organizations where everyone can make a contribution… where everybody counts.. organizations which will continue to change the world.

ELIZABETH DOLE

Tomorrow, who will really care how fast we grew? Isn't it more important to know what we are building with our growth, and why? Measuring more is easy; measuring better is hard. Measuring better requires a clear mission, an exciting vision and shared values.

RON KENDRICK

We're not

managing for the

sake of being

great...we're

managing for

the mission.

FRANCES HESSELBEIN

YOUR MISSION STATEMENT PROVIDES THE WHY THAT INSPIRES EVERY HOW.

CHARLES GARFIELD

WHAT YOU DO DOES MAKE A DIFFERENCE.
EVERY ROUTINE TASK IN
EVERYONE'S MORNING IN-BASKET
CONTRIBUTES DIRECTLY TO
THE ACHIEVEMENT OF THE
ORGANIZATION'S VISION AND MISSION.

DAN ZADRA

Your Mission is meaningful and important not just to your company, but to your community. You can't let it become just a bunch of nice-sounding words on a piece of paper. It must become and remain a clear and compelling call to action.

GIL ATKINSON

We are the echo of the future.

W.S. MERWIN

The problems of the world cannot possibly be solved by skeptics or cynics whose horizons are limited by obvious realities. We need men and women who can dream of things that never were.

JOHN F. KENNEDY

The future
is in the hands
of those who
can give tomorrow's
generations valid
reasons to live
and hope.

PIERRE TEILHARD DE CHARDIN

If we were logical,
the future would
be bleak, indeed.
But we are more
than logical. We
are human beings,
and we have faith,
and we have hope,
and we can work.

JACQUES COUSTEAU

We must stop assuming

that a thing which has

never been done before

probably cannot be done at all.

D O N A L D   M .   N E L S O N

OUR CHILDREN
WILL CREATE A
WORLD
WE CANNOT IMAGINE;
THEY WILL ACCOMPLISH THINGS
WE CANNOT EVEN
DREAM.

KATHRYN T. SHAW

Great teams set
aside personal
agendas to focus
all their resources
on a **common goal.**

AL SCHMITT

Make visible what,

without you,

might perhaps

have never

been seen.

ROBERT BRESSON

DECLARE YOUR MISSION —
AND THEN LIVE IT!

TOM WELCH

CHERISH YOUR VISIONS,
YOUR IDEALS,
THE MUSIC THAT STIRS IN
YOUR HEART...
IF YOU REMAIN TRUE
TO THEM, YOUR WORLD
WILL AT LAST
BE BUILT.

JAMES ALLEN

Also available are these spirited
companion books in The Good Life
series of great quotations:

drive

friend

heart

hero

joy

moxie

refresh

service

spirit

success

thanks

value

welcome

yes!